1993

You are always —
beyond everything —
So of course this book
had to be for you —
Love L

I
realize a
concern for nature
is in fashion, a kind of
ecological chic. It is easy to
talk about rescuing the earth, but
so long as we cover it with garbage
and debris, nothing is going to change.
I want to pay attention to all material—
even plastic—to redeem the forgotten. I
want to rescue the rejected, to combine
it with natural elements, stones, shells,
flowers, dead or alive. Rejected or
rescued. Rejected and rescued: it
is all part of our visual
environ- ment.

GERD VERSCHOOR

beyond flowers

Collecting & Arranging Natural Objects

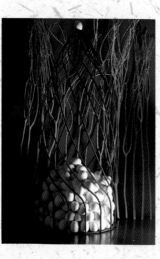

WRITTEN WITH
BO NILES

PHOTOGRAPHS BY
KEITH SCOTT MORTON

STEWART, TABORI & CHANG
NEW YORK

Published in 1992 by

Stewart, Tabori & Chang, Inc.

575 Broadway, New York, New York 10012

Library of Congress Cataloging-in-Publication Data

Verschoor, Gerd.

Beyond flowers : collecting & arranging natural objects / Gerd

Verschoor ; written with Bo Niles ; photography by Keith Scott Morton.

p.   cm.

ISBN 1-55670-181-0

1. Table setting and decoration.   2. Flower arrangement.

I. Niles, Bo.   II. Morton, Keith Scott.   III. Title.

TX879.V47   1992

642'.6—dc20   91-37806
                               CIP

Distributed in the U.S. by Workman Publishing,

708 Broadway, New York, New York 10003

Distributed in Canada by Canadian Manda Group,

P.O. Box 920 Station U, Toronto, Ontario M8Z 5P9

Distributed in all other territories by

Little, Brown and Company, International Division,

34 Beacon Street, Boston, Massachusetts 02108

Printed in Japan

10 9 8 7 6 5 4 3 2 1

To Rob Houtenbos

Thanks

ACKNOWLEDGMENTS

My very special thanks for realizing
this book go to:

Susan Bergholz, New York

Pino and Jessy Luongo, New York

Le Madri Restaurant, New York

Biene Burckhardt, Stevensweert,
the Netherlands

Howard Estrin, New York

Mirella Virgili, New York

Sonja and Richard Moens,
Amsterdam

Alecia Beldegreen, New York

Angelo Bonita, Washington, D.C.

Margaret and Don Stern, Orient,
New York

Dutch Flower Line, New York

Piet and Lynn Lozer, New York

Simon Doonan, Barneys New York

Mallory Andrews, Barneys New York

Mary and Jim Lynch, Dell City, Texas

Kristian Schwendt, Vienna

Bo Niles, New York

Keith Scott Morton, New York

Lynn Pieroni, New York

Jennie McGregor Bernard, New York

beyond flowers

The countryside where I come from,

in the eastern Netherlands near the

little village of Zwolle and the sea,

is called *het vlakke land,* or "the flat

land." Here, nature seems to repose

upon the vast expanse as upon a great

table. Trees, grasses, tulips, stones are

rooted in flatness and the sky

overhead rests upon these natural

things as softly as it does

upon the sea.

≈

We lived, my family and I, in a modest

stone house surrounded by a large

garden fenced in by bushes. We had an apple orchard, raspberries, a kitchen garden where we grew our own vegetables, and flowers. To me, even as a child, the natural landscape seemed a structured form of art. My toys were sticks and stones. I made little landscapes inside shoeboxes.

When I was about seven or eight, I wanted to create a landscape of my own that would be bigger than a shoebox. I wanted a garden outside in nature, a real garden planted with flowers and vegetables chosen by me. Things around me began to take on meaning, and I wanted to make something in nature that would be all mine, separate from anything belonging to my brother and sisters.

Each year, during my mother's spring cleaning, we children were given cracked cups and saucers which we were allowed to break. It was an exciting and shocking ritual. I didn't know it then, but you never really have the opportunity to really see something until you break it on purpose. To see what it was or had been, and then to see what it becomes, is a shock. To look at the pieces, the shards, and remember the shape of what they had been and, at the same time, study their shapes now, and imagine the shape of what they could make:

this excited me, even though I didn't quite know why. Breaking those cups showed me that everything can have more than one "beginning."

Of course, I could not articulate exactly what I felt then; I only knew I wanted to make something of my own, not from something new, but from the colors and textures and forms that already existed in nature.

And so that summer,  I made my first garden, in a corner of the yard, with marigolds. I loved marigolds. I loved their vibrant color, their pungent freshness, their round forms. I loved their bright and sunny softness as much as I loved the shiny, brittle hardness of the broken cups and saucers. I loved how marigolds grew easily, no matter how I scattered their seeds. I loved how nature gave them to me, to grow or smell or cut for bouquets.

Even then—as a child, planting my marigolds—I knew I had to remain involved with flowers. I knew I had to make arrangements with them, and with all the wonderful things I found around me in nature. I knew I wanted to compose with nature, to create art with natural materials.

In the Netherlands one must study for four years to become a florist. When I turned eighteen, I found my chance to do just that. To earn my tuition, I awoke very early each day and delivered milk. I then attended school throughout the day. I worked again at night. I was so excited by the flowers I accelerated my studies and completed them in two years.

After a three-year apprenticeship with a florist, I bought my own little shop. It was just a tiny cellar, but it was located in Kampen, a historic town to which people come on weekends from all over the Netherlands. To attract these visitors—to catch their eye—I wanted to make my shop something special. Every two weeks I painted the shop over, completely, inside and out, each time using a different color. And I sold flowers only in that same color. I had no other decoration.

I followed the seasons to cue my flowers and my colors. During March, of course, I chose tulips. All summer long, I gathered armfuls of wildflowers from the fields and from the side of the road. In the autumn, I filled my store with chrysanthemums; in winter, my palette was white.

At first, as I had been taught, I created big bouquets of these flowers. But soon I discovered that the more deeply I explored the color and shape of each flower, the more I could not cut it just to make it look nice in a bouquet. I became obsessed with the idea of cutting and would lose contact with the flower. Sometimes I would cut and cut and cut until only the head remained.

Gradually my bouquets evolved into what curious passersby called "strange arrangements." I could no longer limit myself to flowers. I was excited by the many different kinds of objects I found in nature: rocks, stones, wire, grasses. Debris. I put these into my "bouquets." I mixed stones with grasses, and plastic blossoms with so-called "traditional" blooms. I joined them by shape, connected them by color, married them by texture. Composing with nature, I created a new "nature" of my own.

I asked myself: What lay beyond the flowers? What was the essence of their being? What could I do with them, with all the elements of nature I discovered as I collected and rummaged, with the materials I found there, after they had already been used? Flowers are beautiful when they are fresh: why are they called ugly when they are no longer new? What could

Beyond Flowers

I do to make the ugly beautiful, to make a still life still have life, beyond flowers?

~

The more I asked these questions, the more I became removed from the shop. I then began to experiment as a performance artist, creating my own landscapes, going beyond flowers as bouquets into flowers as art.

By refusing to confine possibilities to the predictable, "new" kinds of natural forms began to open up to me: dried petals, torn stems, desiccated fruits, lichen-encrusted stones, branches stripped from their trees by the wind, shells washed onto the sand. Paper. Plastic. Metal. Bricks. The discarded. The forgotten.

What happens, for instance, when plastic, made by man, is penetrated by nature? When, abandoned by the road, the edges of a plastic flower turn green from the rain? What can I do with it when its color changes, when it acquires its gentle veil of mold? How does nature affect an object left behind? What is its new beauty?

After leaving the shop and performing onstage for a year or two, I received an invitation to construct a landscape onstage, in Amsterdam, for a group of visiting American designers. They said, "Come to America." I thought then that this is where I must be. To experiment. To find possibilities. I went first to Washington, where I remained for a year and a half, and then to New York, where I began to create arrangements for Le Madri restaurant in the Chelsea district, and for Barneys New York department store windows.

~

I came to America to see things differently. I want others to see differently too. To notice the unnoticed, to perceive the unperceived.

I want others to see the luxury of simplicity that informs the ordinary, the humble, commonplace things. Everyone needs these things in their lives, yet when they are no longer new, everyone rejects them. Everyone wants things that are lovely, but they need the courage to honor the ugly too, and see the beauty beyond the surface.

I don't want to follow fashion. Instead, I want to encourage people to break the code of convention. I want people to invent their own interior, their own landscape, their own table decor—arrangements that will reflect all the creative and wondrous facets of their personalities.

In this book, I want to show how to re-create the feelings of an unforget-table day, how to re-create the atmosphere of a special event in a composition of collected objects that brings back memories of that day. Browsing, rum-maging, collecting form the basis of memory, and of decision. What to save? What to salvage? What to scavenge?

Once everything is collected, how do we put everything together, how do we assemble these wonderful things so that they will allow us to see their beauty? When the objects are collected into a composition, what will the arrangement say to us?

Rummaging calls for special decisions. To buy something unusual in a flea market, pick something up off the street, scavenge in the woods, or pull some-thing down out of the attic is a challenge to discrimination and taste. Will it be color that informs the choice? Will I choose, today, everything in sun-bright hues, like my marigolds of long ago? Or will texture guide the selection? Will crusty things, like bricks and lichen-embroidered stones, draw my eye, or smooth things, like shards of cups, or grasses?

Another challenge—and problem—of collecting is: when to stop. The excitement builds because there are more and more treasures waiting to be discovered, some to use today, some to arrange later on—perhaps some never to use at all, but merely to enjoy as is.

What is more irresistible than bringing home objects from the outdoors that were a witness to our enjoyment of nature? Arranging the objects will take you back to that particular excursion, will keep alive a fleeting sensation, a singular and special moment of pleasure.

I want you to feel free to do as you please. I want you to dare to resist rules and conventions, fashions and trends. There is only one rule for me: Break-through. Break through habit and custom. Dare. Arrange. Rearrange. Combine. Startle. Surprise. You will find that once you begin, this will become a passion, and you will surpass yourself.

Introduction

The Seasons

spring

Spring: What does the season mean

to me, to us?

For some of us, spring means

blossoms; for others, scents,

fragrances, smells. For me, it means

bright green, as well as a different

feeling to the air.

When I was a child, my mother used

to say to me, "When spring comes

and you feel butterflies in your

stomach, then you are ready

to change."

We know that spring signals the

beginning of a new cycle in nature.

Most of us are so tired of winter. We are tired of the darkness, the barrenness, the cold. With spring, days lengthen, trees bud, the sun begins to feel warm.

Suddenly, unconsciously, we begin to make plans. Even in the city I can feel the difference. In spring, I open wide the windows in my apartment to feel the fresh, new air. I put on my spring clothes and shut away the weight of winter. Like  spring, I am constantly changing. It's almost like being in love—my blood tickles and I feel like smiling all the time.

To me, spring means that nature is exploding all around. Flowers, buds, blossoms, blooms, grasses: everything jumps out of anonymous places, frozen wintry places, in such amazing variety it takes my breath away.

I also have the feeling that time is short, and that I must try to enjoy as much of the explosion as I can absorb. I want to drink in this energy, this abundance. I want to be out-of-doors as much as possible, and so I begin to make plans to go away from the city for the weekend. As spring catches and takes hold, I want to catch spring's blossoms. I want to see the cherry, the dogwood, blooming bright pink and white against young green leaves. I want to bring a branch home into my living room. I want to show that spring is here, in my house, as well as outside.

Not everyone is able to cut a branch from the new season. But there are other ways to make a change, to discover, to rediscover spring's recurring newness.

~

Start with spring cleaning. My mother always did. Everything in our house had to be moved outside, into the garden. Every closet and every cabinet was cleared.

Throughout the year my mother would save broken and damaged cups because she did not want to serve her friends coffee in cups with missing shards. She collected the cups in a closet for a special reason and a special person: my grandmother. My grandmother came every spring to visit and help my mother with the spring cleaning. We children always looked forward to her visit. We thought she was a little crazy because she would take all the cups and throw them against the old brick wall in our garden. One by one, she threw them, and we children, my sisters and brother and I, joined in. To her, this was the way to get rid of winter, to begin a new cycle. We loved it. How else could we break something on purpose?

One year, when I was about eleven, I asked my mother if I could have the broken cups instead of giving them to Grandmother. At first she thought I wanted to have all the fun of breaking the cups for myself. I told her that instead of breaking them, I wanted to do something different with the cups. Of course, I had to convince my brother and sisters to give up the treat of breaking the cups with Grandmother, but when I explained what I wanted to do, they went along with my plan.

I took a plywood board, painted it black, and placed all the cups on it in a cluster. Then I glued them onto the board. I asked my mother if I could hang the cup board on a wall in the living room. She said yes. My cup collage hung in my parents' house for a long time.

≈

So, in spring, I like to rediscover what I've collected over the years. I like to look at the mismatched glassware or odd ceramic that has been buried over the winter in the back of the closet. I don't throw anything away. Everything contains its own newness, its own recurring cycle, its own beginning—its own "spring." There is always another use for the old, the broken, the forgotten.

I think of this as a bit of folk wisdom, to combine an object with its own metaphor, to look at an object for its associations with its own past, and, like nature, with its own re-  curring cycle. I take this as a challenge: to open my mind and my eyes to new ways of perceiving things, especially in the spring.

On the first beautiful weekend in spring, I find many natural "leftovers" from the cold season just past—frozen, wrinkled, damaged squashes, for instance, or fungus—the decayed detritus that conveys the hardship of winter. I like to recycle their winterness into the newness of spring by making a new composition with them. I use these things as a transition from one season into another, from the bleak and dead and cold to the colorful and alive and warm.

During these first warm weekends, to visualize new beginnings, I go to places that will clear my head. I find a brickyard, for instance, to be a source of inspiration. Sometimes I go alone to these out-of-the-way places, and sometimes I take a friend with me. We look and we talk about what we see, what to take home. A friend will often have a different and just as special point of view that will spark ideas.

I like to browse, and see the shapes and forms that piled-up brick or stone takes on. Sometimes an unusual piece of wood or metal catches my eye and I bring it home.

What is in the flower market? When I go to the market in the spring, I always feel inspired to gather things, especially flowers, and especially tulips, which come from my country, the Netherlands. I like to gather them in great bunches, and then I like to add something to them, some surprise. I like to put things together that seem to have nothing in common, no connection at all to each other. Or I like to put things together by common sense, to see how they relate to each other. That way I create a new still life, a new spring.

Spring

31

*b*efore spring begins to leaf and become green, I like to take a walk in the fields to remember seasons past and to see what is due to arrive soon.

On a sunny day in a hayfield, I found bales of hay abandoned and hurtled here and there by the stresses of winter. I was reminded of the freshly cut hay of my childhood, when we used to make slides in the haystacks. Seeing these bales of hay, I was inspired to play with them as an adult. I created a long wall with the hay bales, in effect making a room for the new grasses that will grow there. The land, no longer bare and abandoned, is ready for spring.

Trees stripped by winter are also ready for spring. Soon the sap will rise from their roots to their limbs to nourish new leaves. But for now I can enjoy their shapes, the tangle of tendril and twig which makes a black mesh in front of the sky. Soon that mesh will fill with green, with leaves.

*i*n spring, my eye finds its own rhythm, its own perspective, as it adjusts to great and small shapes. Sand, found in many places—at the beach, in the desert, at a brickyard—makes wonderful landscape forms. Here, at a brickyard, piles of sand simulate deserts or arid mountains. The blue sky and warming sun that signal spring define the crusted curves of this earth which has been frozen with cold and which now begins to shift and heave and change with the winds brought by spring.

*I*n the fields, the snow melts away and reveals a beautiful simplicity. Rows of squashes, abandoned from the fall harvest, dried and desiccated by the cold, rest upon the softening ground. A wooden snow fence divides the canvas of the earth; a naked tree holds the horizon. Try to notice these natural compositions, for their integral beauty, and for the inspiration they may provide.

As the season begins, I am ready to browse through the streets and the markets *(below)*, to see what I can collect for new still lifes. Flower shops and nurseries bulge with flowering bulbs such as tulips and daffodils and hyacinth. Gather up as many flowers as you can—as if you were in a garden. You can always put your flowers in a vase with water; try to add something to the bouquet to make it different.

In Dutch still-life paintings of the seventeenth century, the tulip always appeared at the top to show how important it was.

Inspired by these paintings, I created my own still life *(right)*. I tied bundles of broom fibers around a tall glass vase, in which I placed tulips. Just as in a true Dutch painting, a tray of fruit and bread completed my composition.

Spring

37

Often, for various reasons, we throw things away. Perhaps a saucer is broken or a plant has lost its green leaves. When this Dracaena plant *(left)* lost many of its leaves, I kept the skinny plant instead of throwing it away, and settled it among other house plants. I added some green snowballs, or Viburnum, balanced green cabbages on the rim of the Dracaena's pot, and rested a cabbage alongside.

Instead of planting spring seeds in containers and anxiously waiting and watching each day to see when they will grow, "plant" a simple bouquet of flowers in a bucket and enjoy them just as they are *(above)*. I did this on a friend's terrace: I immersed a bunch of tulips in a bucket of water and placed a Philodendron behind the flowers both to surround them visually and to act as a parasol.

We all have things around the house that basically seem to have nothing in common. We use these things here and there, or, more likely, we store them in disparate locations so we cannot easily find them.

One day, a friend of mine who is enamored of metal came to my house for tea. I wanted to make her feel welcome, so I assembled a tablescape for her from all the metal things I could find. In the kitchen I have a teakettle designed by the architect Michael Graves. In the cupboard I found a baking pan and a silver serving plate and two metal cups which fit perfectly on the plate. As I rummaged through my closets I discovered a piece of a car motor that I had retrieved from the woods. And, finally, in my studio, I picked up my metal briefcase.

I used the briefcase as a container by inserting a small vase inside. I chose nigella flowers because their soft green and pale blue hues look so compatible with metal. I added more green, the color of spring, by combining plastic leaves with two round green peppers in the baking pan. Finally I covered a branch in thin soft gray rubber to contrast with the shiny gray metal. When my friend came, she was very touched at my display, and we spent the afternoon catching up with each other, each drinking tea from a metal cup.

Spring

*D*uring one of my first trips out-of-doors one spring I came upon a dormant vineyard *(below)*. All the grapes were gone. All the vines were gone. All that was left were the poles used to support the vines. Depending upon where I stood I could visually shift the poles; sometimes I could only see a few and sometimes all the poles were in view.

When I returned home, I translated the regularity of the rows of poles in the vineyard into four square collages of sticks *(right)*. I cut the sticks the same length, and then filled each square more and more, as if the sticks were coming more and more into view.

The same idea of shifting angles, or perspective, became the background for some green barley I found later in the season. I tied the barley into a sheaf and placed it on top of a table to dry out by itself. I added a green coffeepot and also a stone covered with moss—to capture the feeling of two seasons at once: the cold dry one just passed with the alive, moist, warm one now unfolding.

Spring

*i*n spring
anemones come into bloom. These
spirited flowers vary from white to red
to blue to purple. I am often seduced
by their colors, yet I invariably decide
to buy a bunch of one color at a time.

It is easy to create a still life around
one color. When I came home with
purple anemones, I decided to make a
purple tea party. Instead of using a
tablecloth, I unrolled a blueprint given
to me by an architect—its colors also
unfurl from blue to purple.

I found the purple-banded tea
service at a flea market. The anemones
look wonderful with the teapot, sugar,
and creamer, especially with two tall
narrow cylinders of wood standing
guard on either side of the bouquet.

To celebrate the spring holiday, Easter, I made a still life in golden browns, the colors of the awakening earth. I did not want to use flowers because everyone gives flowers for Easter. I wanted to limit myself to simple things that, to me, suggest new beginnings.

I had saved some bulbs from the autumn, after allowing their leaves to shrivel back into the bulbs. I had pruned them clean and hidden them in the back of a dark closet to await the new planting season. I left the cobwebby roots intact, protecting them with some shreds of brown kraft packing paper.

First I lay the kraft paper on a table and then set a square mirrored tray on top. I filled an Art Deco vase with my bulbs, spreading out the beautiful roots like a nest. Two Champagne flutes became vases for a pair of dried artichokes and more torn strips of kraft paper furl behind as a wavy backdrop. To welcome the holiday, I included two bird nests and a woven straw chicken with a bright red beak.

You might not equate a brickyard with nature, nor a junkyard, but, for me, nature is everywhere and embraces everything I see out-of-doors. A brickyard or a junkyard or an abandoned lot can be natural sources of inspiration for shapes and forms and patterns *(below)*.

At the beach *(right)* I created a huge driftwood sculpture by pushing a branch through the open knothole of a stranded log, which I then stood upright where the sand meets the sea. My "signpost" points the way to new ideas.

Spring

49

vintage vitrine *(left)* which had once showcased a quartet of cakes graced the setting of a theatrical production in which I had been involved. I resurrected the vitrine after the play closed and hung it on my wall to give my pair of aqua ceramic pheasants a place to perch. Pieces of green pottery matched their color and fit perfectly within the box. To complete the scheme I felt Viburnum blossoms suited best.

This thick plastic molded slab with eight pockets originally protected the parts of a light fixture. I retrieved it from the trash, and now I use the slab over and over, most often as a serving tray for crudités. Sometimes, as a centerpiece for my table, I float individual blossoms in pools of water in the pockets *(above)*.

Interlude

queen's throne

Every year on April 30, we Dutch celebrate the birthday of our queen. The celebration was initiated to honor Queen Juliana, who is now the queen mother. Our present queen, her daughter, Beatrix, continues the tradition by honoring her mother's birthday instead of her own. Because the queen has decreed this, for her word is law, we still celebrate on April 30. In the Netherlands, the queen's birthday is a holiday, and everyone has the day off. The entire country celebrates with festivals and plays. We all love our queen—and her mother, too.

Even abroad, the Dutch get together on this day. In New York, where I live now, we gather at the Dutch consulate and sing our national anthem, drink orange bitters, a traditional liqueur, and eat herring. On this day we all feel very Dutch.

To honor our queen, I created a throne for her birthday. Our monarchy is very old, and so is the chair I used, which I found in a flea market. The chair dates from the seventeenth century. At first I did not know what to do with it, but after seeing the queen's annual address to her nation, which is called the "Speech of the Throne," I had an idea for a composition in her honor: a chair and a robe. The queen wears a robe with a long, long train when she makes her speech, and her throne has a canopy, so I created a long, long moss robe for her throne.

I wanted to create this throne as a souvenir, and as a special reminder, for I have met the queen. A few years ago, when I still lived in the Netherlands, there was an important art exhibition held in that country. All the leading artists in the world were invited to be represented there. The committee that organized the event asked me to create a bouquet to welcome the queen. I knew that Queen Beatrix loves art. I proposed to create a special bouquet for her, and this is what I made:

I found clear plastic tubes and I rolled

leaves inside each tube. Then I gathered them together and surrounded them with a bunch of plastic flowers. I held the bouquet together with cellophane that had been printed with pictures of baby's breath, and I tied it all up with lots and lots of bright blue ribbon.

Queen Beatrix responded kindly to my proposal, even though the committee was unsure how she would react when I presented it to her. She said, "I want to meet the artist who dares give me this bouquet." First I was screened by her security force. They instructed me how to behave. You cannot go up to the queen and simply ask her something. You must wait until she addresses you, which she did, so kindly. She asked me why I wanted to make this bouquet for her.

Whenever our queen goes out in public she usually wears a dress printed all over with flowers, so I answered her question, "Your Majesty, a more beautiful bouquet than the dress you are wearing I could never dare create, and since you are a powerful woman, I wanted to make a statement for you which would not compete with your good nature. So I used plastic instead." I proved to her that something that seemed useless or unattractive at first could, from a different standpoint, be very pleasant, both to look at and simply enjoy. Her lady-in-waiting told me that the queen liked what I had said and liked the bouquet. She took it home.

And so, here in New York and here in my book, I want to honor the kindness of my queen with my composition—my throne and its long, long train of soft, soft moss.

summer

Summer: The season of maturing powers, of longer days, the season in between spring and autumn. Trees become greener and greener, the rich color of their leaves deepening as they mature. We need to be out in the sun because the sun gives us new energy. I love the Dutch expression *volwassen*, or "maturing of powers," for this means I can allow everything I find to mature, to transform itself into something new. This season, summer, prepares its bounty for survival. Summer means abundance, of many things mixed up together. I feel full of abundance; I love to walk on the city streets with an enormous bunch of sunflowers—holding them, just to feel and see them, to have contact with them. And to make other people see them too.

Summer is the season when so many flowers bloom. The flower that catches my eye the most as springtime ends and summer begins is the rose. Like the tulip is to spring and the chrysanthemum is to autumn, the rose— to me—is the flower of summer. The rose is the queen of all flowers. Like the season in which it blooms, the rose has many associations and meanings. No other flower is so written about, so often mentioned in song. The rose is the flower for lovers or for those about to fall in love.

Once roses were so prized, so valued as an expression of feelings, they were dried and served to be eaten. Their petals were pressed into rose water. Thousands upon thousands of fragrant and fragile petals were necessary to create one single, tiny vial of this precious liquid. Bulgaria is still renowned for its rose water and every year celebrates the rose in special festivals throughout the countryside. Every street is blanketed with rose petals. In the Middle East, rose water is sprayed in the living room when guests are due, and a drop of rose water is added to many foods, as an enticement and as a gesture of courtesy.

What I love best about roses is that after enjoying them in a beautiful bouquet, after their petals curl and their fragrance fades, I don't have to throw the flowers away. I take them out of their water and hang them upside down to dry, to save for another time, another place.

You can do this with  so many of summer's offerings, such as herbs and Queen Anne's lace, and with so many materials of summer, such as gourds, fallen tree bark, and seashells. The summer takes care to make its materials endure, many of them through drying, to prepare its bounty for later on. This is the season to collect as much as you can, to save everything, so that you will be ready for autumn and for winter.

As summer approaches I start to think about vacation. I want to spend a short time in a part of the world different from my own. I want to discover a new culture, a new place, another form of art. Now is the time to do something we normally don't have time for, to take a rest from our everyday life; this is a time of being outside, visiting new places, taking pictures, bringing home souvenirs.

Souvenirs can be so many different things: a doll, a vase or plate, a piece of fabric, a rock, a shell, even sand from the beach. Taking home something from another corner of the world transports us back and forth, in time and place, into memory and back again. We all have vacation experiences and memories. We want to show our friends where we have been, what we have done, what a good time we had. Sometimes I see something, a reminder, and in a flash I receive a memory of where I have been, someplace else, someplace distant.

I often bring home natural things that were previously unknown to me, that interest me. This is what fascinates me so about nature; everywhere you go it is so different.

On one of my vacations I visited Panama—my first trip to an exotic country. The first thing that I noticed were the colors, all the different greens, and the fruits and flowers that I knew only from pictures. I visited a spot at the edge of the Pacific Ocean where the beach was completely black—black sand. I couldn't help myself and immediately filled a sack with handfuls of sand. At my friends' home, where I was staying, there was to be a dinner party that very evening, and they asked me to take care of the table decoration. The table was set up outdoors and it was made of glass. I decided not to use a cloth, not to cover up the shimmering glass, but to place a mound of the black sand in the center of the table. Then I went outside and started to collect whatever I could find in the neighborhood. I found a piece of bark from a huge palm tree, and dried coconuts, and palm fronds. The fronds I made into place mats, and the coconuts and bark were gathered upon the sand.

The guests were surprised; they had never thought of these materials as decoration because they were so commonplace. But I looked at these things for their shape, for their color, for their form, and with that point of view they became new and different—exciting, even.

On another trip I traveled by car to Italy. I started my drive in the north-east of France, in the mountainous region of Alsace. As I traveled from village to village on my way south, I started to collect. And I kept collecting—twigs, stones, wildflowers, pinecones—through the mountains and forests of Switzer-land, and on into Italy. By the time I arrived in the little Italian village where I was to spend my vacation, my car was full. I checked into my hotel, but instead of suitcases, I brought in box after box, filled with my collections. The owner looked at me strangely. I knew only one sentence in Italian, so how could I explain? I settled into my room and began to arrange my collections here and there. The next day, the owner's assistant came to me and laughed aloud: *"Miracoli; che bellezza,"* or "Miracles; how beautiful." Everyone was so nice to me in the hotel I decided to create something for the entrance to the hotel, as a welcome for the guests. I made a little landscape using all the stones and twigs and flowers that had dried during my drive, and assembled them on a table by the front door. I wonder if it is still there.

I love to revive memories by taking souvenirs of nature from my vacation place into my home. I look at what I have collected. Shells from beaches far away, from as far away as Panama, or Italy. I like to make a collage of my treasures, to initiate and inspire a conversation with friends, to show that I, too, am always, like nature, changing.

In this season of maturing powers we can show off our changes, and allow the differences between us to bloom. In summer anything is possible.

Summer

Walking along the beach, I keep my eye out for treasures that have washed up onto the sand: a salt-scrubbed piece of driftwood, thick curls of seaweed, the claw of a lobster or crab, shells broken (or, less often, intact), creatures robbed of their succulent flesh by relentless gulls, waterworn shards of glass—objects I can recycle now that their natural cycle has passed. Usually I gather what I like best in a bag to transport home, but occasionally I rearrange what I find, just where I find it, into "beach-pictures." I leave these behind for someone else to see—or for the rising tide to pull back into the sea.

uring the summer I like to cut as many grasses as I can, for this is when they are at their longest and greenest. It is best to crop grasses early in the season, before the sun becomes too strong. Sun and heat rob the grasses of their sap and color. After I cut the grasses, I hang them in the open air to dry. I am always on the lookout for rain, though, for once grasses are shorn and separated from their roots, they cannot tolerate rain. When the grasses look and feel right, I make arrangements with them both indoors and out. Sometimes I stand them upright in a simple frame I made from pieces of weathered wood; sometimes I lean them to one side; and sometimes I just play with them and groom them as if they were long, long hair. When the grasses are left like this, they will dry naturally and will last for a long time.

Every day, I try to exercise my sensibility to the things around me. I set a little challenge. I select some objects that I may have ignored or neglected, and look at them closely to visually feel their shape and texture. I think of how they might be used in a composition. What will happen, for instance, when I work with three vases encrusted with green paint, vases I am accustomed to seeing filled with flowers and set out on a freshly-dug grave? Rubbed clean of their paint, the vases emerged as clear, clean metal cones, pure sculptures. Placed upon the table in front of the stick collages I made in the spring, they gleam in the slanting sunlight. *Hosta sieboldiana* leaves in chemical beakers provide a perfect counterpoint of color and form.

*i*deas sometimes arrive when you least expect them, but you can create a mood for them if you allow yourself to relax completely. To me, taking a bath invites such a mood. Bathing can be a kind of ceremony, an indulgence, which I honor by creating a landscape or scene that will involve and soothe me as I relax in the warm water. The always-resilient grasses accommodate my design. Tied together in bunches and lined up, like a private marsh, they allow me to contemplate their beauty. By adding a row of little plastic alligators to the scenery, I add a little bit of fun and whimsy.

A sunflower is the most extravagant, and yet most conservative, of flowers. It turns its full face to the sun and absorbs the sun's rays like a sponge, creating seeds rich in nutrients. Gardeners vie with each other to see who can grow the tallest plant, and the one with the largest head. How can I do this flower justice? What objects would enhance its brilliant yellow? Summer squashes, perhaps, and onions. I decided to dramatize two blooms, and the linear stateliness of their plucked stems, with a collection of squashes stood vertically in a glass bowl with onions grouped in another bowl alongside. Brown cardboard and a bird of paradise provide the backdrop.

or an informal meal, I wanted to dress up the table in an unusual way. With such an epicurean delicacy as crab on the menu, it first occurred to me to set the table with a white tablecloth—but I quickly rejected this idea as it was too reminiscent of a restaurant. My green china banded with gold—china which I've bought piece by piece at flea markets in the neighborhood—would look too ordinary, too plain arranged on such a tablecloth. I wanted to make the most of the color green, so I cut a piece of rubber matting, the kind normally used to cover and protect a kitchen floor. It was a lovely green, the same as my plates. Then I stood a gold party hat at each place setting, as a podium for each crab, and I dropped a claw or two in each dish. For a little more green, I spray-painted some leaves. The cutlery, small hammers and saws, was provided to divest the crabmeat of its pitiless armor.

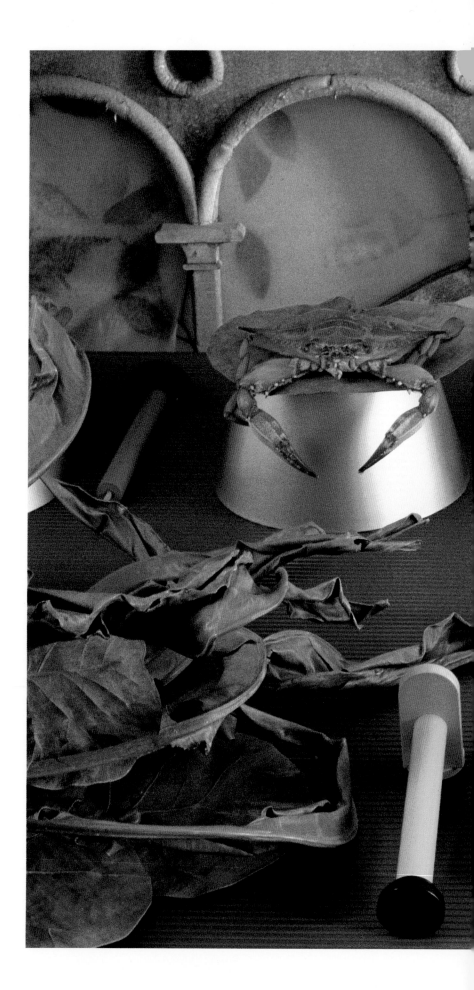

Beyond Flowers

*I*t is a common axiom, almost a cliché, to say that art imitates life or nature. Here, in the studio of a good friend *(left)*, I decided to turn the cliché inside out. As soon as I saw the painting of artichokes flying like leaves across the canvas, I brought in artichokes of my own and arranged them in homage to the art. With their stems removed, they are immobile, while their painted counterparts appear to dance.

On a table set at the edge of an inlet *(above)*, I wanted to experiment with shapes and textures. The shape and weight of these watering cans, with their long triangular spouts, set up a tension. To balance them, I "filled" them with artichokes. If allowed to dry for two or three weeks, the artichokes will start to bloom with beautiful purple flowers.

*f*or a small
summer supper at home, I combined
flowers from the garden with flowers
of the sea—irises with feathery coral.
I was inspired by Vincent van Gogh,
who loved irises as I do. The frame of
a lampshade stripped of its tattered
silk became the armature for my
centerpiece. I upended it on the table
and thrust in the corals and a few
bundles of grass, which firmly held
the irises in position. Around the base
of the centerpiece I scattered crab
shells which I had rescued from the
beach. The soft pinks of their shells
combined well with the intense
yellows and pale purples of the irises.

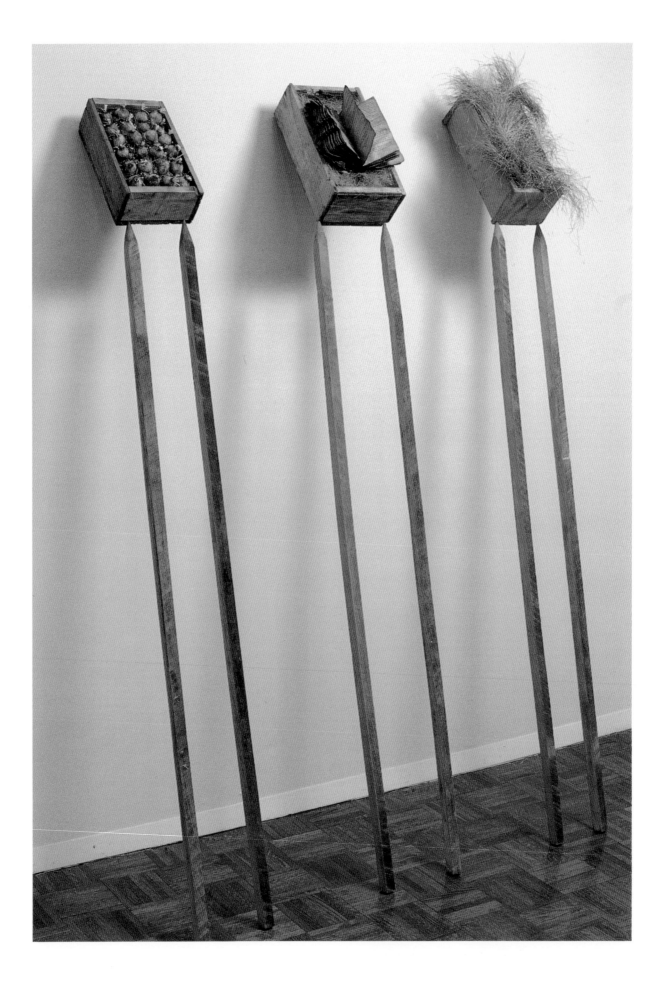

When I collect things I am never quite sure how I will recycle them. I just know they are all there, in my closets, waiting and ready for my ideas. I found a wooden box filled with dormant spring bulbs, and a box of dried spring grass. On one of my trips out-of-doors, I discovered a faded, water-stained book which described the leaves of various trees. Many poets write about nature, so I decided to make a poem with nature, with the bulbs and the withered grass, the book, and three boxes supported by six long tomato stakes. The contents of each box speak of the beauty that once was, when the bulbs and the grass and the book were, in effect, in their season, and of the beauty which still exists, now that the cycle of nature has run its course.

*t*hroughout the year I return again and again to the beach. A beach is like a natural collage, yielding layer upon layer of objects. Sometimes I follow the line of the tide, where the wet sea has deposited its latest treasures upon the dry sand. Sometimes I wade right into the foamy surf. Many things may not appeal at first, but nothing should be ignored. Something which doesn't interest you at first may work well in an arrangement or collage. The process of choosing is not always obvious, so collect enough to allow for inspiration.

As summer progresses, nature changes. The leaves, so delicate in spring, become increasingly opaque. To me, tall green grass, purple hydrangeas, and green grapes *(left)* in a pale green wooden container suggest these changes. The long grass gives an exuberant feeling to the entrance hall.

Late summer, anticipating harvest, offers such abundance, such variety. I love the sweet delicacy of Queen Anne's lace *(above, left)*, the long, thin green beans of the catalpa *(above, middle)*, or simply as many flowers as possible *(above, right)*.

*f*rom time to time as I drive through the countryside, I am seized by a moment in nature and in time. Here *(below)* I was caught by the slant of early evening light across a series of barn doors. For me, the light was power, the power of nature. To represent this, I moved three long poles against the three doors. The simplicity of the forms and the light and the colors isolated, and connected me to, the stark beauty of the moment.

Two weathered fence posts and hydrangeas plucked at their peak were combined in a simple, natural arrangement *(right)*. I rested the two posts against a barn, angled them toward the sky, and inserted the colorful blossoms into the empty holes. During the fall, all will fade—wood and blooms alike—merging to an elemental grayness that signals the inevitable approach of winter.

Interlude

green grass

There is a phrase: "The grass is always greener on the other side of the fence," or, as we say in the Netherlands, "Your neighbor's grass always grows greener." Is that true?

The Netherlands is well known for its green grass, and, because of that, for its healthy cows, which give delicious cheeses. But this doesn't mean that the grass anywhere else in the world cannot be as green. Grass is known throughout the world, not only on land, but in the sea as well.

There is a tiny grass in the Netherlands that we call the "shoe-sole plant." This is a grass that originated in Italy. In ancient times, when the Romans made their marches north to conquer Europe, they walked over sandy, unpaved tracks. Unconsciously, they trod upon the grass in the tracks or roads and flattened them into the sandy soil. As they marched, they carried the seeds of this grass on the soles of their shoes. After a few years this little grass was spread throughout Europe—thus, the shoe-sole grass.

Grass is a very strong plant, a survivor. Some people call it a stubborn weed, since it is so difficult to destroy. Grass also can be very beautiful. As a child, I loved to browse through the grass. When we plan a picnic, don't we look for the perfect spot carpeted with lots of lush, thick, green grass? Is it the grass that attracts us, or its green color?

There are so many varieties of grass, and it grows in so many colors. In wetlands it looks pale, almost yellow; in moist earth it is intensely green; in the desert it seems almost gray. And even the same grass changes its mood with the season, saturated with color during the spring, desiccated during the arid summer. Grass is a barometer of weather and place. Some grasses hug the soil, some soar and sway in the wind. We are so used to seeing grass around us, we sometimes forget it is there.

Before I came to America, I ran a workshop to teach people to look at and observe nature in different ways. Because I love grasses, I persuaded one group of fifteen students to follow me to Switzerland for one week, to search for and gather grasses and work with them there, on the spot. I rented a bus and we drove to a little village outside Zurich. We stayed in the only hotel in town, and the owner gave us his basement to work in.

In the morning we drove out into the countryside to cut the tall meadow grasses we found there. I told my students to cut the grass into bundles and secure them with rubber bands. Because grass shrinks as it dries, string cannot hold it tightly enough.

Returning to the hotel in the afternoons, we made laundry lines on all the balconies adorning the façade of the hotel so that we could hang up the grass to dry. The villagers gathered in front of the hotel and gazed at the grasses and asked what was going on. We had a talk with the owner of the hotel and agreed to have an exhibition of our work in the little square in front of the hotel.

I asked my students to make landscapes out of the grass, by weaving them on a loom. Almost like painting, the blooms on the grasses were woven to create another dimension against the flat weave of the grass landscape.

On the day of the exhibition the villagers and neighboring farmers began to arrive by tractor, bicycle, horse and wagon. Some of the women came in their work aprons. They had never seen an exhibition in their village, and certainly not one constructed from these materials. Why did we come all this way to work with grass? To them, grass was a plague to their fields. They believed it absorbed food and water from other plants.

After a while, they gave in to their curiosity and began to ask questions. The owner of the hotel was so pleased with the attention that he brought out some wine, and we all joined together in a farewell dinner. The table decorations, of course, were made of grass.

Everyone, students and villagers, was happy. How beautiful it can be when you see things from a different point of view.

fall

Fall: The third season of the cycle, the
time to share the fruits of nature. This
is the season when we realize and
enjoy the results of summer's maturing
powers. It is the time of harvest.
Fall evokes a deep respect for nature,
for the cycle of growth, which then
leads into the cycle of decay. And
decay evolves from full ripening, into
replenishing, into nature's giving
abundantly of herself, to us. Fall
shows what we can learn from growth
and from growing things.

∼

The air is different, it has a different smell. The humidity of summer has dissipated: the air is crisp. The sky is clear. All the greens, so tender during the spring, so lavish during the summer, are shifting, altering, diffusing their translucence into opacity, into yellows and reds and oranges, and finally browns. The trees and grasses are ready to rest, too, to retire.

When fall arrives, I go outside to feel the wind. I take long walks in the woods or along the beach and let the wind play with my thoughts, with my memories. I am not  ready yet to give up the outdoors; I am not ready to stay inside. I want to stay out as long as possible. We all have a favorite season, and every season is different. For me, fall is the most exciting because it is the last chance to save and collect for the coming winter, the season of rest.

$\sim$

Walking outdoors in the fall, it feels good to look everywhere and capture in your eye, and in your hands, what you see. Look at the sunflowers, now that their heads have drooped and are heavy with seeds. Look at the squashes, both ripened and rotted. Look at the fat pumpkins and the ripened corn. Gather in what you can. Save as much as possible.

The head of the sunflower is like a mosaic. Two sunflower heads can rest upon a table as a centerpiece, like two tightly tiled disks.

Look at a cabbage. It is like a bouquet of flowers. Pull back its outermost leaves and rest it, too, upon a table or windowsill or shelf. Mix an armful of green cabbages with red ones.

Pick up the fallen leaves and let them dry. Leave some upon their branches and strip others away. Look at the shapes of the leaves, of oaks and maples, for instance, and see how they curl as the days go by.

≈

As a child in the Netherlands, I used to go into the woods with my father to collect berries for the marmalade my mother made every fall. I always carried an extra bag to collect whatever I could find on the forest floor, just for myself. Back home, while my mother's pots simmered on the stove, I opened my bag, upset its contents on the floor, and started to make my own treasure, my own little woods. I took an old shoebox and all the stones and twigs and mosses and mushrooms that I had collected; inside the box I created a bed of the colors of nature—green and gray and brown. When I finished, I cut a little hole in the front of the box and glued a piece of colored cellophane, like a pane of glass, over the hole. I also cut a few holes in the lid so light could enter my woods. I showed my landscape to my parents. We shared this indoor woods for a long time.

I also used to walk in the woods with my grandmother. I admired her because she knew so much. Walking with her was always exciting and a little scary because she could go deep into the forest and never get lost. She seemed to know each and every tree—especially all the walnuts. As we walked we gathered the nuts that had fallen onto the ground. We filled our baskets to the top with walnuts, and also with mushrooms, and a few pine needles. Back in our kitchen, we shelled the nuts, carefully so we wouldn't break them, and then she put all the nuts into a jar. She took about half a pound of sugar and added just enough boiling water to cover it. Then she poured the sugar water into the jar over the nuts. She cleaned the mushrooms and washed the pine needles and put them into the jar too. Last she reached into the back of her kitchen cupboard and brought out an aged bottle of cognac. She opened the bottle and poured all of the cognac over the nuts and water and mushrooms and pine needles. "This is for the long winter nights," she said, smiling.

My grandmother also made an autumn dinner from the walnuts that remained. She bought cheeses from the farmers nearby and grapes and wine. Again, we would peel the  shells and skins from the walnuts, then eat them, like that, with the cheeses and grapes. Now, when fall arrives in New York, I remember my grand- mother by putting to- gether this same meal. And I still make her wal- nut liqueur. And walnut pralines. I take the two halves of each walnut and put a bit of almond paste between. Then I melt chocolate and roll the walnuts in the chocolate. After they cool, I eat them. They taste heavenly! Walnuts and memories of my grandmother: this is my Thanksgiving.

Because fall is the season of maturing, I think often of the old people—like my grandmother—whom I have known. I think of people who are in the autumn of their lives. People who know and understand the fruits of their experience, like my grandmother, and the grandmother of my closest friend, who lived in a castle. On Sunday afternoons we would visit her. I asked her, "Why do you live in a castle? Only kings and queens live in castles, not grandmothers." And she answered, "Everyone likes to have a front yard and a backyard." Her backyard was a park with a lake and a forest.

In her castle was an enormous attic, stuffed to the rafters. Like me, my friend's grandmother was a collector. She collected everything, from ice cream scoops to plastic flowers. I loved to make arrangements with her things. After she died, I went back and collected all the plastic flowers that were in her attic and created an homage to her, in her memory.

Fall

97

i love grasses in many different ways. I love them when they are barely unfurled from their seed in spring and again when they stand thick and tall and lustrous in the summer sun. Here, in the fall, I cut and re-cut dried grasses and carried them in armfuls back out-of-doors, to repose gently upon the earth from which they came. Instead of using a string to tie them, I wrapped them in an old wisteria vine. I like the contrast of the airy, vulnerable grass and solid, resilient vine.

I enjoy butternut squashes *(above)* for their luxurious shapes and the playful combinations they make when grouped together.

I used butternuts in counterpoint to a soaring ceramic seagull I had picked up at a flea market *(right)*. The wings of the gull and the squashes composed their own dialogue of curves. I introduced more white ceramics to complement the seagull and the squashes—a vase, filled with dried *Celosia cristata*, or cockscomb, lace, and a coffee set. The soft folds in the white silk background echo the rigid folds of the vase. The composition allows for an interplay between nature and design, contrasting yet complementary.

repetition and multiplicity. Patterns recur over and over, shapes and forms are everywhere if we only stop to look and consider. During the fall, elements in nature, drained of life, assume a brittle profile, and man-made objects glint in the harsh, cool sun. Pieces of slate make jagged angles against the sky; tractor tracks etch thick patterns into the hardening soil; stacks of concrete blocks resemble high-tech sculpture; coils of chicken wire are piled in circles of shadow and light.

On a trip to Florida I watched an enormous palm tree being cut down to make way for a high-rise condominium. I salvaged as much of the tree as I could, and shipped five large pieces of the palm back home. I then stripped and split the stems of the leaves and leaned them up against a stairwell *(left)*. They remind me of the beauty the tree had represented in nature.

I also salvaged dried coconuts from that same palm tree and made them the focus for a cocktail party *(above)*, combining them with candelabra made of rusted iron. The tonal allure was striking in the soft glow of candleflame.

Fall

Here the leaf stems of the salvaged palm tree become more sculptural, less decorative. I created this arrangement as an homage to the palm—a visual token of my respect for its strength and grandeur; of my admiration of its nobility and slender, swaying majesty; and of my thanks for the voluptuous, shady retreat it provided from the blistering midday sun, for the cool, refreshing breezes it provided beneath its verdant canopy. Robbed of their former vitality, the stems appear to hunch together mournfully and lament their fate as they lean against their wailing wall.

Corn is a universal nutrient—like potatoes and rice. Corn feeds the people of many nations, both in body and in spirit. In the Southwest, people hang clusters of corncobs outside to please the gods of harvest. Here I honor corn in a composition with an Italian vase from the 1960s.

ature's canvas is everywhere.
Illuminated by the golden rays of the setting sun, frilly-edged lichen
creates an abstract painting on a gravestone on Long Island.

*t*ime has thrown its broken veil over this graveyard monument. A testament to the process of nature, the mustard-brown tones of the lichen contrast serenely with the cool gray granite.

Fall

I I I

baroque bouquet of leftovers celebrates the bounty of summer that I amassed in my collections: hybrid delphinium, dried hydrangea, celosia, or cockscomb, amaranthus, squashes, and hearts of sunflowers *(left)*. For me, this is the last burst of energy and autumnal color before winter's stillness. The bouquet will dry out completely, and thus last for a long time.

A trip to the cemetery in the fall crystallizes for me the intensity of the cycles of the seasons *(above)*. "Ashes to ashes," we all return to the soil. The stones absorb and hold tight to the warm rays of the sun. It is peaceful here, magical. I think of the lives of beloved ones resting under this soil, returned, like grasses and flowers, to nature's embrace.

i don't always bring everything I like home, especially during the fall. I like to feel and look at and think about the objects I find—right at the spot where I find them. This helps me consider what to keep and what to give back to nature right away. This is the way I train my eye.

A small skeleton, for example, looks wonderful right where I found it, as does this collection of tangled sticks and vines *(below)*.

After the autumn drains life-giving sap from plants, it often leaves in its wake long, long strands of vine. I pulled away many compliant vines and carried them home. Still flexible, they yielded to my twists and turns as I tied them into a sculpture *(right)* which I placed on top of a birch log. I tethered it to itself, top to bottom, with a rubber–wrapped electrical cable I found in a field.

The sunflower offers us so much in every season. We can hang it outside to feed the birds; we can extract nutritious oil from its seeds; we can also use its precious blooms in artistic endeavors. Van Gogh painted sunflowers. Here I created a sculpture with them.

I had owned this chair formed from strands of strong wire for many, many years. I could not throw it away even though it needed two legs and a cushion. One day I looked at my collection of sunflowers from the summer and I thought: one of these blossoms must be the perfect size for a cushion for my chair. It fit perfectly and, in fact, appeared as if it had been embroidered especially for the seat. The sunflower also offered its stem, cut in two, for two legs. Now the chair is complete and has found a new life in my studio.

On a visit to the Netherlands, I returned to the castle which belonged to the grandmother of one of my close friends. I wanted to bring a gift as a souvenir of thanks for all the special time I had spent there over the years. Carnations, so plentiful during the fall, are also overcultivated and overused and, as a result, their beauty is often overlooked. I wanted to bring attention to their beauty once again, and so I placed them along the edge of the widest stair to the castle. That way, when people stepped over them, they would be obliged to look down and regard these humble flowers with a fresh point of view.

*D*uring this same visit, I wanted to call attention to the majestic shape of the volutes, which flank, midway, the castle stairs. Upon them I laid a bouquet of very old silk roses. The timeless beauty of the roses, delicate, fragile, emphasizes the massive, permanent form of the stone scroll.

$\mathcal{S}$torms and winds and frost have removed all the leaves from the trees, and transferred them to the cold ground where they will decay and offer new life to the soil. Now—when the trees are bare and we can see further into the woods—is the season of the hunt. To honor this, I placed my stuffed pheasant on top of a post covered with feathers and vines *(above)*.

As autumn fades into winter, I clear the ground by gathering twigs and branches. These I tied into long, tapered sculptures *(right)*. Together they draw attention to the muted tones and sharpened forms of the season.

Beyond Flowers

Interlude

tumbleweeds

A child sees the world from a unique point of view. For me, growing up in the Netherlands, the name "United States of America" had a magical sound and meaning.

When I was thirteen or fourteen, I saw my first cowboy movie. Until then, like many small boys, I had devoured books written about these heroes from the United States. I wished we had cowboys in the Netherlands. I dreamt my own cowboy world, full of adventure: with my friends we made up situations from the books we read.

In my parents' attic was an old chest filled with my grandparents' old clothes. We used my grandfather's hats, hats that were way too big for us, but we could pull them down over our eyes so they gave us the perfect dangerous look we were after. From my grandmother's discarded old fur coat we cut little strips and glued them under our noses. We made guns from wood and horses from brooms. My parents' yard was our prairie.

We also made ourselves into Indians. One time we needed lots of Indians for a big scene. We colored our skin with light-brown shoe cream for a warlike effect. Then, of course, we needed lots of feathers. We pulled the tails of all my father's chickens. The chickens squawked and were very upset, and my father was too. He thought his egg layers had an illness; why would they all suddenly lose their tails?

I was very impressed by that first cowboy movie, but also somehow disappointed. How different it was from what I had been imagining. Yet, in these same movies, I also saw, for the first time, those strange twiggy "balls" rolling through abandoned streets and towns. What were they? Why did they always come with a huge wind?

When I came to the United States, I was determined to hunt for tumbleweeds. But where to start? I looked at a map, and El Paso had the magical sound of the cowboy movies I had seen.

Two friends came along, too. Arriving in El

Paso was a shock. In my imagination it was a sleepy little town where men rode on horseback. And here was a six-lane highway running through the center of town. People laughed at us, and some didn't even know what a tumbleweed was. We decided to rent a car and just start driving. After a couple of hundred miles we saw a huge sign: Downtown Cornudas. Home of the Famous Texas Burger.

All of a sudden, we were there. Downtown Cornudas. Beside the road were a little café and motel. The "city" had four inhabitants; the motel owner was the mayor. We moved into the motel, so we immediately booked the entire town. And that evening we ate the Famous Burger.

We talked to the mayor about our search, and she started looking under one of the tables in the dining room. With pride she showed us a faded newspaper, the *Dell City Courier*. It showed a lady next to a Christmas decoration made from a tumbleweed. We telephoned and made an appointment with her for the next day.

Dell City is about fifty miles from down-town Cornudas. It feels as though it is in the middle of nowhere. The streets are unpaved. The people speak with a thick accent. We found the lady in the newspaper; she turned out to be the editor of the *Dell City Courier*. She was very excited that we had come to see her.

Immediately she called her husband. He was a real cowboy, but instead of coming on a horse, he came in a truck. They drove us to their ranch. I'll never forget my first sight of the tumbleweeds: I couldn't stop touching them. I felt like Alice in Wonderland. Here I was, all the way from the Netherlands, and I'd found my tumbleweeds. We loaded up the truck. I'll always remember the feeling of driving that truck with my treasures piled up in back. We drove back to Dell City. When we unloaded, everyone stared at us.

We learned that people use tumbleweed to fish, by putting Texas Burger inside it. They drop the tumbleweed into the water with a line and, if they are lucky, crayfish are caught inside. Maybe now people will see tumbleweeds from a different point of view.

winter

Winter: The last season, the season of
recollection and reflection. The season
of nature's rest. Winter is the time
when nature shows her nakedness.
Trees have lost and scattered all their
leaves in the fall storms, and flowers
are not growing anymore.

~

During the winter I like to go outside
again, even in the cold, to see what
nature in this season offers. I walk in
the bare, abandoned fields where what
is left over tells me what must have
been. The remains I find there, of

squashes or other growing things, seem very vulnerable to me. They are frozen in their decay, their softness made hard by the cold.

As I walk, I look around me at the trees. Naked branches reveal the shapes of trees to me, shapes that seem more real in a way than when the trees are fully dressed with leaves. Winter is the time to look at nature's true forms.

For some, winter means cold days with nasty weather and frozen streets, a time to remain indoors. For others, it means celebration and the holidays.

After Thanksgiving I love to shop, for now the streets are illuminated and festive and I hear music everywhere. All around me people are smiling. There is a feeling of warmth, in spirit and in the air, even in the icy cold. We begin browsing for a Christmas tree. Where do we want to put the tree this year? Will we decorate it in the same way as last year? We start thinking about how we want to decorate the house. Some like it glittery and colorful; others decorate in a more modest way. Always, though, the ornaments and the decorations are very special. For me, the holidays mean: green, light, pinecones, wreaths, candles. And the thought: What can I show my friends that will be special this year?

$\sim$

When I was a child, I always looked forward to Christmas Eve. On that night we children would dress up as angels. We made wings out of palm leaves, from our houseplants, and we made little wreaths, our halos, out of straw. Then we would join the children from our village and gather to sing carols at the big tree which had been raised in the village square. From there we would go into every café, singing,  and the customers gave us change or bought us cups of hot chocolate.

Later, my mother would stay home to decorate the house, while we would go to church. It was very exciting because our Christmas service was held at three o'clock in the morning. We were awakened and dressed in the dark, and then walked in the deepest black night to church. All the while the church bells were ringing, and it was often snowing.

After church, we went home, where my mother was waiting for us in front of a beautifully decorated table set with our Sunday china and crystal glasses. On the table stood masses of little red tulips in pots wrapped in green paper. Our tablecloth was always white.

We drank hot chocolate with brandy in it, and for dinner my mother served a traditional warm sausage and stollen. After the meal we had a glass of hot, spicy wine. Imagine, all this happened at six in the morning!

Then my mother brought us around the beautiful crèche carved by my grandfather, which she placed on top of a low cabinet. She set the crèche in a bed of moss and greens to make a landscape for the Holy Family to rest upon. We sang carols, and then, at eight in the morning, we all went back to bed to sleep.

≈

I like to remember those Christmases from long ago, but I also like to make my own landscapes in a different way. For me, Christmas means birth, beginning. So I like to make arrangements in my house with paper-whites, the little white flowers that announce the new cycle of nature that will soon begin. Paper-whites link me to the coming season of spring, and, although spring is still distant, I am happy to know I can be sure to find its precursor at Christmastime.

Winter

Winter, the season of hibernation, drained of color and vitality, holds a special secret: I know that nature, composing itself for a new cycle, has drawn deep into itself, concentrating its juices in roots and veins. The holidays remind me of this—Christmas pines, cut and tied in bundles on the sidewalk, emit their rich, tangy scent into the cold air. Strolling the streets in search of a Christmas tree for my home, I sniff and revel in the perfume and touch the sticky sap. Soon I will unwrap my chosen tree and decorate it, but I also appreciate the trees as they are, tied and tethered as beautiful tapers.

Nature's colors and shapes are honed by the tough winter sun into distinct studies in survival. Now, when all is hushed and still, I bring my own offerings into nature: stones arranged on a weathered piece of wood *(top)*, and rusted cans, seaweed, and a length of brown velvet composed upon a solitary log *(right)* are gifts of my inspiration. Sometimes, I just contemplate what nature created without my help *(middle and bottom)*.

*b*lack is the color of winter's dark days. Into the darkness of an arrangement of black materials *(left)*, I introduced the unexpected—an enormous bunch of green bananas.

Four weeks later the bananas turned brown, rotted, and dried, leaving behind a spiny skeleton which I revised for a new still life *(above)*. Here I dangled a piece of wood from a crate that had washed up on the beach against a scrim of thin rubber. In front I lay an old coconut hull to continue the scheme of muted colors. The banana spine I let slink out, like a snake, from a metal box which once contained a movie reel.

During the winter, with so few flowers in the market, and, of course, none in the garden, we must rely on our imagination for substitutes. I look for opportunities inside my closets, in shops, and on the street. In a store near my home I discovered a long tube of cups, the kind made for water coolers. Upside down, and arranged in a square to echo the shape of the plates, their conical forms made a delightful (and inexpensive) table decoration, reminiscent of the snowy peaks of a winter mountainscape. It is fun to use something so common and familiar in such an unexpected way.

*f*or me, the
holidays are a time for honoring
traditions. I remember Christmas at
my mother's table—set in Christmas
colors of white and red and green—and
I return to this palette when I create my
holiday centerpieces. In the Netherlands, red tulips signify many things,
including a prediction of spring; I like
to mix them with waxy gardenias
which offer a special gift of scent. For
green I add *Asparagus plumosus*, so
common as a filler for bouquets from
the florist, but a surprise here used as
frothy petticoats for the blooms. Holly
berries grace each place setting.

During the holidays I pull out my collected pine cones and place them in various empty spots around my apartment. These I nested with unfurled strips of birch bark in a basket crafted of cedar twigs. Asparagus ferns provide just the right touch of green *(above)*.

In the Netherlands, we celebrate the holiday with Christmas tulips, grown especially for this joyful day. Here *(right)* I clustered bunches of perfect red tulips in a bright, white tureen, along with achioté and holly berries. The layers of buds were cut from nascent palms, reminding me both of the Birth of the Child and the birth of a New Year.

Beyond Flowers

*b*unches of thin ribs from the cycas tree find their way into many still lifes because of their acquiescent linearity; they comply with my demands, yet retain their integrity in every arrangement. Here, a thin bundle hangs gracefully against one of a series of metal panels on a studio wall.

Cycas ribs repose behind a still life of damaged squashes which had littered an abandoned field. The squashes, left over from the summer and now completely dry, had lost their flesh and bulk, but, surprisingly, not their shape. Fragile, and linked to the cycas ribs by mottled monochrome, they find new life in a paper bucket accented with drapery fringe.

reen, the color of growth and vigor, of spring and summer, the color of Christmas. To emphasize this *(above)*, I placed a wide bundle of gardening stakes tied with copper and an old Danese Italian vase filled with artificial greens against a backdrop of green tissue. A gothic window symbolizes the holy spirit of this season, while the green and blue lights signify the celebratory.

A feathery, winglike branch of *Araucaria heterophylla*, or Norfolk Island Pine, arcs over glowing votive candles and rows of pomegranates *(right)*. A piece of tin ceiling hangs behind, as beautiful and spiritual in its decay as any stained glass window.

*f*ruits in various
stages of ripeness and decay reflect
the passing of the seasons in an
unexpected, burnishing shaft of
afternoon sunlight. Two huge pine
cones, secured to a pair of candlesticks,
guard the mélange of fruit like twin
trees, or sentries. The ripe fruit can be
eaten, or left to dry further, to be used
in other still-life arrangements.

When I venture out-of-doors during the holidays, I am uplifted by the sights and scents and sounds of the season. My eye discovers the visual gifts of winter's festivities everywhere: a stone angel crowned with a colorful branch of holly; tangled branches of smilex spilling wildly from their encasement; aisles of blue spruce Christmas trees awaiting purchase on the sidewalks; a putto gaily dressed with a wreath of pine, baby's breath, and red and gold ribbons.

Winter

153

i like to dress my table even when I expect no guests, to give the tabletop life and imagination. This is the season when the shops are filled with the supplies of holiday gift-making—styrofoam balls and cones and wreaths. Instead of adding to the conical "trees" I found, I simply painted them to emphasize their geometry. To give the holiday arrangement some movement, I added a festive crinkle of green and blue tinfoil.

One of the ways to see—and see again—is to present a form or object in multiple, as I did on the top of a chest of drawers with small bundles of kindling. Although the bundles represent the promise of warm winter fires, they are beautiful on their own. They also provide the joy of the unexpected—who would expect to find kindling on a tabletop?

The green pheasants, which I use in various ways throughout the year, are the centerpiece for a table decoration in shades of green *(left)*. Swags of greenery and bunches of silver brunia garland the birds and two angel candlesticks. Instead of candles, since they are everywhere in the house at this season, the angels carry pine cones.

After Christmas passes, I cannot bear to hide my ornaments away from view. Like the bits and shards of nature's bounty I hoard and use all year, an ornament or two can be recycled, and observed over and over in new ways. I rest a large shimmery blue globe upon a window sill to complete an unplanned still life *(above)*. The jewel-like reflection conveys a special sentiment of celebration and hope into the New Year and beyond.

*t*he holidays come at the end of the year and herald the arrival of the next. I don't want to relinquish all the special feelings of one season, even though I want to look forward to those of the next.

We must endure a couple of months of barrenness and cold before spring arrives, but there are ways to bring the season into the house ahead of time. So many spring flowers can be nurtured at home, especially from bulbs which have been resting quietly just for this occasion. To me the first messengers of spring are the paper-whites. I create a final arrangement for the year with them, and in so doing, start my cycle of collecting and imagining and dreaming and creating all over again.

Design by Lynn Pieroni

The text for this book was set in Bauer Bodoni, composed in-house
on a Macintosh IIsi by Barbara Sturman, and output on a
Linotronic L300 at The Sarabande Press, New York, New York.

The special backgrounds were reproduced from handmade papers:
The Seasons: sugar cane paper by Dieu Donné, New York;
Spring: Blumenfield paper by Twinrocker, Indiana;
Summer: floral paper by Tut Neyar, Israel;
Fall: Kasuri rice paper, Japan;
Winter: Chiri bark paper, Japan.

The book was printed in five colors and bound in kraft paper
by Toppan Printing Company, Ltd., Tokyo, Japan.

Production by Katherine Rosenbloom